Learning to Read, Step by Step!

Ready to Read   Preschool–Kindergarten
• big type and easy words • rhyme and rhythm • picture clues
For children who know the alphabet and are eager to begin reading.

Reading with Help   Preschool–Grade 1
• basic vocabulary • short sentences • simple stories
For children who recognize familiar words and sound out new words with help.

Reading on Your Own   Grades 1–3
• engaging characters • easy-to-follow plots • popular topics
For children who are ready to read on their own.

Reading Paragraphs   Grades 2–3
• challenging vocabulary • short paragraphs • exciting stories
For newly independent readers who read simple sentences with confidence.

Ready for Chapters   Grades 2–4
• chapters • longer paragraphs • full-color art
For children who want to take the plunge into chapter books but still like colorful pictures.

STEP INTO READING® is designed to give every child a successful reading experience. The grade levels are only guides; children will progress through the steps at their own speed, developing confidence in their reading. The F&P Text Level on the back cover serves as another tool to help you choose the right book for your child.

Remember, a lifetime love of reading starts with a single step!

*To Mark Fredrick McKissack, the newest
member of our family —P.C.M.*

For Tessa —S.S.

Text copyright © 2005 by Patricia C. McKissack
Cover art and interior illustrations copyright © 2005 by Sanna Stanley

All rights reserved. Published in the United States by Random House Children's Books, a division
of Penguin Random House LLC, New York.

Step into Reading, Random House, and the Random House colophon are registered trademarks of
Penguin Random House LLC.

Visit us on the Web!
StepIntoReading.com
rhcbooks.com

Educators and librarians, for a variety of teaching tools, visit us at
RHTeachersLibrarians.com

Library of Congress Cataloging-in-Publication Data is available upon request.
ISBN 978-0-593-43276-1 (trade) — ISBN 978-0-593-43277-8 (lib. bdg.)

Printed in the United States of America
10 9 8 7 6 5 4 3 2 1

This book has been officially leveled by using the F&P Text Level Gradient™ Leveling System.

Amistad

The Story of a Slave Ship

by Patricia C. McKissack

illustrated by Sanna Stanley

Random House New York

In August 1839, two officers on a Coast Guard ship spotted something strange in the waters off Long Island. It was a ship, long and black. It was flying a Spanish flag. And its name was *Amistad*. In Spanish, that means "friendship."

What was so strange about the ship?

Its sails were in shreds. There was no captain. The ship was just drifting, going nowhere. And a group of black men were on deck yelling.

What were they doing? Why had the ship come to New York? Who were the people on board?

The officers decided to find out. So they rowed out to the ship. They did not know that they were now part of one of the strangest and most interesting stories in American history.

The story began many months earlier
in Sierra Leone on the west coast of Africa.

AFRICA

 Sierra Leone

 Mende tribal area

A man named Sengbe Pieh (say: SANG-bay PEE-ay) lived in a small village. He belonged to the Mende (say: MEN-day) tribe. Sengbe had grown up in a round house with a grass, cone-shaped roof.

Later on, he built the same kind of house for his wife and three children. He was a wealthy rice farmer, a leader among his people.

One day, Sengbe was taking a walk
alone. Suddenly, some men surrounded
him!

Sengbe fought to get away. But the
men had guns. They were slave catchers.
They were kidnapping him.

Sengbe was dragged into the belly of a slave ship. Hundreds of men, women, and children were packed inside. The ship was bound for Cuba.

Chained together in the darkness like animals, the people cried. They begged for mercy. Sengbe thought he would go mad. There was no room to stretch or turn. The smell was sickening.

It took two months for the slave ship to cross the Atlantic Ocean and reach Cuba. Many of the Africans had died. Some had been killed. Some had killed themselves during the horrible trip. But Sengbe clung to life.

What lay ahead? That he did not know. Still, he did not lose hope. He wanted to see his family again. "I will live for them," he told himself. He would find a way back home.

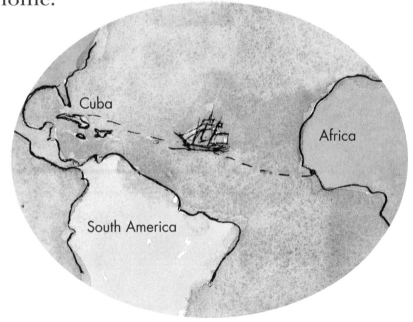

In Cuba, the Africans were given
Spanish names. Sengbe became Joseph
Cinque. Then a few days later, he was
herded onto another ship—the *Amistad.*
It was bound for Brazil on the east coast
of South America. New slaves brought
high prices there.

Cinque tried to tell the sailors that he was not a slave. He and the others were not animals. The captain didn't listen. He whipped Cinque instead.

On board the ship, Cinque told the others to be brave. Be strong. Survive. He would find a way to free them.

In the rotten wood of the hold was a loose nail. Cinque had a plan. He worked and worked to pull the nail out of the wall that held the chains. His hand was bloody and sore, but it was free. He was able to unlock the chains and free his other hand. Quietly and quickly, the other Africans freed themselves.

Under the cover of night, the
Africans attacked. Swiftly. Deadly. They
found sharp knives and killed the captain.
Then they killed the cook. Sailors leaped
overboard. Some escaped in lifeboats.

Only two Spanish sailors remained on the ship. Cinque used sign language. He told them, "Sail us back to Africa or die!"

The sailors agreed. But they had a plan of their own. To return to Africa, the *Amistad* had to sail east. During the day, the ship sailed east toward the rising sun. But at night, the Africans could not tell which way the ship was heading. So the Spanish sailors headed north at night. Day in, day out. The ship zigzagged up the eastern coast of the United States.

United States

Cuba

By August 1839, the *Amistad* had
reached the waters off the coast of
Long Island. That was when the two
US officers spotted the ship.

On board the *Amistad*, the officers asked the Spanish sailors what had happened. The sailors said the *Amistad* was a slave ship. They told how Joseph Cinque and 53 other slaves had killed the captain and taken over the ship. The sailors were hostages. All that was true. But the two Spanish sailors claimed that the Africans had been born in Cuba. That was a lie.

That may seem like just a little lie. But it made a big difference. In 1839 in the

United States, people could still own slaves
in many states. (Slavery didn't end for good
until 1865.) But already some laws put limits
on slavery. It was against the law to kidnap
Africans and make them slaves. That was
exactly what had happened on the *Amistad*.

Cinque did not know about the US laws.
How could he? He didn't even know where
the *Amistad* had landed. But one thing he
was sure of. The Spanish sailors were lying
to the other white men.

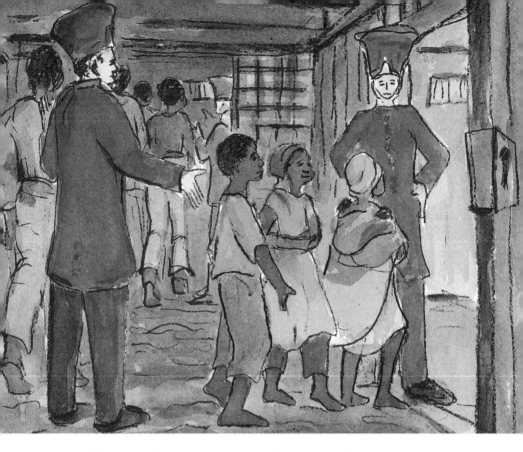

The *Amistad* was taken to the nearest big port. That was in Connecticut. A judge said the Africans had committed a terrible crime. They were charged with murder and mutiny. (That meant taking control of the ship.) A trial was set for September 1839. No bail. Everyone was put in jail in New Haven, Connecticut. Even the children.

People stood in long lines and paid money to gawk at the Africans. Women giggled, and grown men made faces. They acted like it was a silly circus sideshow.

Cinque thought these people were just
as strange. He and the other Africans
turned their backs to them. Alone in his
jail cell, Cinque worried. Would he ever see
home again? He wasn't so sure anymore.

What Cinque didn't know was that
the Africans had friends in this strange
country. Many people in Northern states
believed slavery was a sin. They were called
abolitionists (say: a-buh-LIH-shun-ists).
They wanted to abolish—or end—slavery.

Some abolitionists heard about the *Amistad*. They didn't believe the Spanish sailors' story. If the blacks on the *Amistad* were born in Cuba, why didn't any of them speak Spanish? They must have been kidnapped from Africa . . . illegally.

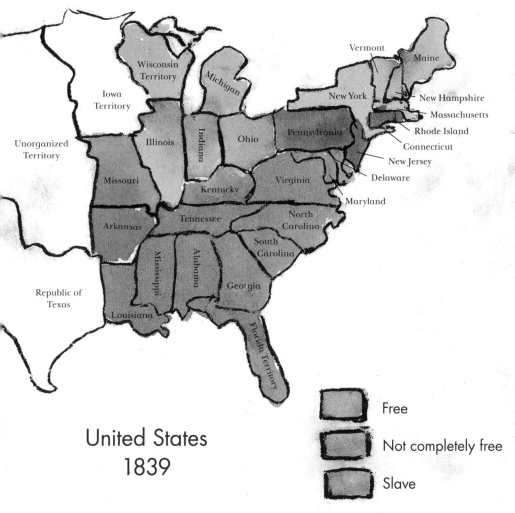

United States
1839

Free

Not completely free

Slave

The abolitionists found a famous lawyer to help the Africans. His name was Roger Sherman Baldwin. He, too, was against slavery. His grandfather had signed the Declaration of Independence.

Baldwin knew the job wasn't going to be easy. First of all, he couldn't talk to his clients. In fact, he didn't even know what African language they spoke.

Baldwin tried using sign language.
That didn't work. Baldwin drew pictures
in the dirt. That was no better. Cinque
knew this man wanted to help. But he,
too, felt helpless.

Then Baldwin learned that Cinque's
language was Mende. That was a start.
He found a black man who spoke
Mende. His name was James Covey. He,
too, had been kidnapped from Africa.
But Covey was lucky. He was set free
and had become a sailor. Through
Covey, Baldwin and Cinque could

finally understand each other.

"We want to be free," was the first thing Cinque told Baldwin. Then Cinque told the whole terrible story.

Yes! Baldwin now knew that the Africans had been kidnapped. This was the heart of what he would say in court.

On January 8, 1840, a trial began. The New Haven courthouse was packed. Baldwin said the Africans were free people. Not property. Not animals. They had been kidnapped. On the *Amistad*, they had been defending themselves. "The same as any man here would," Baldwin said in the crowded courtroom.

During the six-day trial, Cinque and some of the other Africans took the witness stand. They were farmers and craftsmen, fathers and sons, daughters and sisters. They were members of a community.

Cinque told how much freedom
meant to the Mende people. They loved
art, music, and dance. Just as in the
United States, the Mende believed in
laws to govern people. They had judges
and juries.

"We are men, too," Cinque told
the judge.

The judge agreed. He ruled that the *Amistad* Africans were "born free . . . and still are free and not slaves."

What a victory!

Cinque and the others thought the terrible time was over at last.

But it was too soon to celebrate. Their lawyer, Roger Baldwin, had bad news.

The government of Spain insisted that the Africans were their property. It didn't matter what a judge in New Haven, Connecticut, said. Even worse, Martin Van Buren, the president of the United States, agreed with Spain.

What was going to happen now?

There had to be another trial. The Supreme Court would judge the case. The Supreme Court was the highest court in the United States. But the new trial would not take place for another year.

In the meantime, the *Amistad* Africans went back to jail.

Cinque was angry. Still, he told the Africans to be patient. "Do not lose hope."

The people of New Haven were on the Africans' side. The Africans didn't belong in jail. It was dirty. The food was terrible. Some of the Africans fell sick. Fresh water and dry, clean clothes were brought to them. Still, everyone had to stay in jail. Even the children.

Roger Baldwin needed help to win the new trial. It was clear that the president was not going to help. But maybe someone else important would. Baldwin went to see a former president: John Quincy Adams.

John Quincy Adams had been president from 1825 to 1829. He was also the son of President John Adams. Now he was a member of the House of Representatives. He was 73 years old. But his mind was sharp. His tongue was even sharper. And he knew all about the law.

John Quincy Adams visited the Africans in jail. He was shocked at how young they were. "Not one of [them] is over 30 years of age," he wrote in his diary.

By now, two of the Mende people had learned to write in English. They sent a letter to Adams. "Please tell the Great Court our story," they asked.

Adams was moved by their plea for help. He was also very worried. "Oh! How shall I do justice to this case and to these men?" But he would try his best.

Months passed. Many of the sick prisoners died in jail. By the next trial, on March 1, 1841, there were only 37 *Amistad* Africans still alive.

The Supreme Court was in Washington, DC. To win the case, the lawyers had to convince at least five judges that the Africans were not slaves. But five of the judges were from slave states. Would any of them believe the Africans were innocent?

First, the side against the Africans presented its case. The lawyer said the Africans were on a Spanish ship. They were the property of Spain. "They should be returned to Spain for trial."

Next, it was Roger Baldwin's turn. Over three days, he spoke for more than 14 hours! "We are not talking about what to do with a chair or a table, but flesh and blood human beings," he told the judges on the Supreme Court.

Then, finally, it was John Quincy Adams's turn. He was famous as a great speaker. "These men are not criminals. They were defending themselves as

free men." Adams compared Cinque
and the others to heroes in the American
Revolution. Patrick Henry had fought for
freedom. He had said, "Give me liberty
or give me death."

"Was Patrick Henry a criminal?"
Adams asked the judges.

It was very quiet in the courtroom. The
only sound was Adams's booming voice.

"No," he said. "He was a hero."

A majority of the Supreme Court justices agreed. Adams won the case! The *Amistad* Africans were free at last.

When they learned the news, they leaped for joy. Nobody—not even the president—could change the decision of the Supreme Court.

It was March 9, 1841. Two long and terrible years had passed since their kidnapping in Africa. They wanted to show their thanks. They presented John Quincy Adams with a Bible. Inside were the words, "We thank you very much because you make us free."

After all his time in the United States,
Cinque knew English well. He rarely
spoke it in public. However, when it was
time to say his good-byes, his words
were in English. "My friends," he said,
"I thank you all."

Cinque and the others set sail from New York on November 27. The ship was named the *Gentleman*. James Covey, the Mende sailor and translator, returned to Africa with them. They arrived in Freetown, Sierra Leone, on January 11, 1842.

They were home. Home at last.

No one really knows what happened to Cinque. There were reports that he was happy and well at home with his wife and children. Living in freedom again.

In the United States, slavery continued for more than 20 years. It took the Civil War and a Constitutional amendment to end slavery for good. Still, the *Amistad* case gave hope to all people fighting against it.

"We are men, too!" Cinque had said at his trial. His words stabbed at the heart of slavery.